THE SIMPLE SIDE OF

FINANCIAL MANAGEMENT

MANAGING FINANCE SHOULD NOT BE DIFFICULT, BORING OR SCARY

JAN H PIETERSE

For more information, material and advice on many of the topics surrounding management functions go to:

www.NextCEO.co.za

Copyright © 2016 by Jest My Publishing.

All Rights Reserved. No part of this publication may be reproduced in any form or by any means, including scanning, photocopying, or otherwise without prior written permission of the copyright holder.

Additional Action

Go join our Facebook group for exclusive offers, group collaboration, coaching and other great benefits at NextCEOGroupCoaching or follow our Facebook page for general information and motivation NextCEO.co.za

Why I Wrote This Book

I wrote this book because, I felt that in so many cases where people do research studies and/or research papers in general, either for self-enrichment or as part of a study purpose towards a certified outcome, these research papers seem to get lost in the cracks. During my studies I came across a philosophy that stated that; A scholar during their undergraduate degree, merely summarizes and compares the knowledge from the greater pool of knowledge, whereas a scholar studying towards a master degree, searches and tests these collections of knowledge and verifies the information in the greater pool of knowledge, whereas, the Ph.D. scholar is the one that contributes and grows the pool of knowledge.

For many years I believed this philosophy, however, as time passed I realized that even the least expectant individual can significantly contribute to the knowledge pool and feed the inquisitiveness of the information hungry souls. Thus I have decided it a fitting choice to publish the research that I had done for the various business projects during my studies. I can only hope that you would not only find this information useful but that you find the book enjoyable.

Why You Should Read This Book

If you are interested in understanding Financial Management, but you are just not in the mood for those stale academic written, hard to understand, boring textbooks, then this book is just for you.

If you are simply looking for additional information and wish to supplement your existing knowledge of financial management, well then this book is for you.

For the sake of covering both angles, this book includes the academic writing, as well as simpler written interpretations of the same information. The non-academic people amongst us or simply those who will benefit from a simpler side of things can benefit none the less.

With a pinch of salt, a dash of garnish, this book will help you understand some of the in-depth parts of financial management paradigm.

You may at some parts feel that you have completely lost your way, but fear not. As I have, and many before us, you will survive the journeys into the paradigms of the business management empire.

Table of Contents

Additional Action 2
Why I Wrote This Book 2
Why You Should Read This Book 3
Table of Contents 4
Understanding the Book 6
Finance Concepts and principles 6
Financial Management versus. Accounting 7
Five Users of Financial Statements 8
Projected Income Statement 9
Time value of Money 13
Organizational Budget Types 15
Types of Variance 16
Ratio Analysis 17
Cost Analysis 22
Failure Factors 24
Formulations, Valuations, and Calculations 26
Valuation 26
Bonds 33
Cost Comparison Analysis 40
Organization valuation 45
Financial Management in Practice 50
Ratio Analysis 50
Cost-Volume-Profit 67
mergers and acquisitions 69

Forward Market 72
About The Author 73
Other Books By Jan H Pieterse 74

Understanding the Book

The standard text such as this will contain academic style writing with citations and arguments. This is where the facts are defined in great detail. If you prefer to read the fact in their original context, I have included a bibliography at the end of this book for your perusal.

The highlighted text such as this is aimed at the audience that wishes to have a simpler understanding of the topic, and in a way that can simply be retold or re-quoted easily.

Finance Concepts and Principles

Financial management is the heart and soul of the organization. Most businesses have financial reasons as the root cause of their inception. Financial Management refers to the planning, organizing, directing and controlling of the financial activities and the utilization of funds within the organization[1].

What is the difference between financial managements and accounting and what is the use of financial statements in an organization? What is the time value of money concept? These are just some of the questions that cause much confusion amongst managers when approaching organizational financial management.

Financial Management Versus Accounting

Financial management differs significantly from accounting on the basis of financial management focuses on the creation and maintenance of economic value and the importance of cash flow, whereas accounting focuses on whether the business is running at a profit or a loss[2]. However, both these principals are fundamental to the management of business operations.

Simply:

Financial management covers way more aspects in an organization than accounting. Accounting is, in fact, one of the subsets covered in financial management.

Five Users of Financial Statements

a. **Investors**: In order to assess possible risks and anticipated returns[2]

b. **Employees**: In order to assess the employer's ability to provide remuneration, retirement benefits, and further employment opportunities[2]

c. **Lenders**: In order to assess the ability for them to repay loans and interests[2]

d. **Suppliers and Creditors**: In order to assess ability to pay balances owing[2]

e. **Customers**: In order to assess the company's ability to continue doing business[2]

Simply:
Financial statements are useful to various people, each of them has a different purpose for the statement. Investors want to analyze risk, employees may seek assurance in sustaining their employment, Lender may seek to assurance that Suppliers and Creditors may seek information to ensure the organization's ability to pay, Customers seek confidence in companies' abilities to do business.

Projected Income Statement

Given the 2013 projected income statement as below, as well as projected assumption for 2014, a projected income statement for 2014 can be prepared.

Assumptions for year ending 31 February 2014:
1. Projected sales will increase to 4,500,000
2. Manufacturing labor will drop to 20% of direct sales because volume efficiency will more than offset higher wage rates.
3. The cost of materials will rise to 15% of sales because some price increases will not be offset by better utilization.
4. Overhead costs will rise above the present level by 5% while additional variable costs will be encountered at a rate of 10% of the incremental sales volume.
5. Depreciation will increase by 15,000 reflecting the purchase of additional equipment.
6. Selling expenses will rise more than proportionately, by 125,000, because of additional effort will be required to increase sales volume.
7. General expenses will have maintained same levels.
8. Income taxes are estimated to remain at 35% of pre-tax profits.
9. Long-term debt will be set at 5% of sales

JEST Ltd

Projected Income statement for the year ending 31 February 2013

		% of sales
Net sales	3 500 000	100.0
Cost of sales	- 2 200 000	62.9
Labor	900 000	25.7
Materials	520 000	14.9
Overheads	750 000	21.4
Depreciation	130 000	3.7
Gross profit	1 300 000	37.1
Add: Operating income	0	
Gross operating income	1 300 000	
Less: Operating expenses	- 620 000	17.7
Selling expenses	300 000	8.6
General and administrative expenses	320 000	9.1
Operating profit for the year	680 000	19.4
Interest income	0	
Earnings before interest and tax	680 000	
Interest expense	0	
Earnings before taxation	680 000	19.4
taxation (35%)	- 238 000	6.8
Retained earnings	362 880	12.6

JEST Ltd
Projected Income statement for the year ending 31 February 2014

			% of sales
Net sales		4 500 000	100.0
Cost of sales	-	2 607 500	57.9
Labor	900 000		20.0
Materials	675 000		15.0
Overheads	887 500		19.7
Depreciation	145 000		3.2
Gross profit		1 892 500	42.1
Add: Operating income		0	
Gross operating income		1 892 500	
Less: Operating expenses	-	835 000	18.6
Selling expenses	425 000		9.4
General and administrative expenses	410 000		9.1
Operating profit for the year		1 057 500	23.5
Interest income		0	
Earnings before interest and tax		1 057 500	
Interest expense		225 000	5.0
Earnings before taxation		832 500	18.5
Taxation (35%)	-	291 375	6.5
Retained earnings		541 125	12.0

Following the Select, Compare, Evaluate, and Predict financial analysis approach[4,5]

- Sales are up by 28.57% year on year
- Cost of sales is up 18.52% year on year

Simply:

The slower increase in the cost of sales indicates that the organizations is improving on its sales and production processes and contributes to the sustainability of the organization.

This is also reflected in the increase in the Gross profit and Operating profit respectively.

- Gross profit is up 45.58% year on year
- Operating profit is up 55.51% year on year

Simply:

Retained earnings have increased by 22.43% year on year, regardless of the long-term debt incurred. If additional long-term debt is incurred for the next financial year, this increases will decrease but could be absorbed by the further projected sales increase for the following year.

Time Value of Money

Time value of money defines that the current value of money is more valuable than the same money value in the future. This is because money now can earn interest or be invested and earn positive returns, thus being worth more if available immediately[2].

Two of the models of Time Value of Money are:

- **Future Value**: The value at a given future date of a present amount earning interest at a specified rate. Uses simple interest or compounding interest to find future value[2,3].

- **Present/Current Value**: The present value of a defined future value given a specified future date. The future value is discounted at a discount rate to find the present value[2,3]

Future Value

Present (PV) = 15,000
Annual rate of interest (i) = 12% = 0.12
Number of periods (n) = 9
Future Value (FV) =?

$$FV_n = PV \times (1 + i)^n$$
$$FV_9 = 15,000 \times (1 + 0.12)^9$$
$$FV_9 = 41,596.18$$

PRESENT VALUE

Future Value (FV) = 100,000
Annual rate of discount (i) = 15% = 0.15
Number of periods (n) = 5
Present (PV) =?

$$PV = FV_n / (1 + i)^n$$
$$PV = FV_5 / (1 + 0.15)^5$$
$$PV = 100,000 / (1.15)^5$$
$$PV = 49,717.67$$

V (1st year) = 100,000 / (1.15)^4 = 57,175.32
V (2nd year) = 100,000 / (1.15)^3 = 65,751.62
V (3rd year) = 100,000 / (1.15)^2 = 75,614.37
V (4th year) = 100,000 / (1.15)^1 = 86,956.52

Simply:

The time value of money seems to be a concept that few people truly understand, and in most cases people think that interest on loans are charged for the sake of profit, however, since risk free government bonds are in most cases used as the base for opportunity cost, and most banks or other institutions willing to lend money generally takes this into consideration. Thus, if the government bonds offer inflation + 1% per annum return, then any other investment offers a lower yield, is regarded as a loss of income, as the buying power will be reduced over time. There are many other factors which affect the future value of money, and these will be discussed in more details in another book in the Simple Side of Business Management series. With the formula above, the true value of a future amount can be calculated by reversing the effect of the future value formula. In a later chapter, we will revisit these formulas in much more detail.

ORGANIZATIONAL BUDGET TYPES

- **Incremental budgeting**: Budget is primarily based on the previous period's budget or actual results, with small increments made for the new budget[2,6]

- **Zero-based budgeting**: The new budget, disregards the previous budgets and all activities and priorities are re-assessed from zero based on current and future objectives, plans and projects[2,7]

- **Activity-based budgeting**: Focuses more on the level of effort for activities rather than the time spent to execute these activities. Provides opportunities to align activities with objectives[2,8]

> **Simply:**
> The three most popular ways for organizational budgeting is Incremental – just increase last year's numbers, zero based – start from scratch and re-budget everything, and Activity-based budgeting – budget based on grouped values.

Types of Variance

- **Favorable Variance**: occurs when the actual results are better than the expected results, this is denoted with an (F)[2]

- **Adverse Variance**: occurs when the actual results are worse than the expected results, this is denoted with an (A)[2]

> **Simply:**
> Variances are useful and can be used as an aid to measure the effectiveness of an organization, and its effort, it can also indicate performance improvement or decline. Therefore, variance analysis can be regarded as part of an organization's performance monitoring tools. Variances can be used as springboard for further analysis, investigation, and action[9,10]

Ratio Analysis

Net Profit Margin

> Net margin % = (Earnings attributable to ordinary shareholders / Revenue) x 100
> NM = (62136 / 600000) x 100
> NM = (0.1035) x 100
> NM = 10.35%

Simply:
With a positive profit margin of 10.35%, the organization is operating efficiently and indicates to investors the organization's profitability.

Return on Equity

> Return on Equity % = (Net profit / Equity) x 100
> ROE = (62136x 55636 / 464600) x 100
> ROE = 0.1337 x 100
> ROE = 13.37%

Simply:
The ROE indicates that the shareholders earned 13.37% profit on their equity investments in the organization, indicating that the equity base of the organization is being utilized effectively[11].

CURRENT RATIO:

Current ratio = Current assets: Current liabilities
CR = 321000: 131400
CR = 2.4: 1

Simply:

The CR indicates that the organization has a strong current ratio, however, does not reflect an accurate state of the organization's liquidation and should be supplemented with the Quick ratio for a more accurate indication of the liquidity[11].

QUICK RATIO:

Quick ratio (Acid test ratio) = (Current assets − Inventory): Current liabilities
= (321000 − 176000): 131400
= 145000: 131400
= 1.10: 1

Another expression of the Quick Ratio formula is[11]:

QR = (Trade and other receivables + Short-term investments + Cash and cash equivalents) / Current liabilities
= (120000 + 0 + 25000) / 131400
= 145000: 131400
= 1.10: 1

Simply:

According to the result of the QR, the organization can meet their short-term liabilities, but have very little room for any additional liabilities and should do an effort to increase their liquidity. Even more refined would be the Cash ratio to identify the organization's cash liquidity[11].

DAYS' SALES IN INVENTORY:

Days' sales in inventory = (Avg Inventory / Cost of sales) x 365
= (((176000+204000)/2) / 415000) x 365
= ((190000) / 415000) x 365
= 0.4578 x 365
= 167.11

Simply:
There are 167.11 days' sales in inventory, indicating the ratio at which an organization turns inventory into sales, thus this ratio indicates that this organization is holding almost 6 months' worth of inventory[12,13,14].

AVERAGE COLLECTION PERIOD:

Average collection period = (Accounts receivables x 365) / Sales
= (120000 x 365) / 600000
= 43800000 / 600000
= 73

Simply:
Average collection period of 73 days, for all accounts receivable[12].

AVERAGE PAYMENT PERIOD:

Average payment period = Average creditors / Average purchases per day.

$$= ((118900+178700)/2) / (((415000+38500)/2) / 365)$$
$$= (148800) / ((400000) / 365)$$
$$= 148800 / 1095.89$$
$$= 135.75$$

Simply:

Average of 104.57 days for the organization to make payments[12].

TOTAL ASSET TURNOVER:

Total asset turnover = Total turnover / Total assets
$$= 600000 / 716000$$
$$= 0.84$$

Simply:

The organization produced 84c profit for each R1 invested.

DEBT RATIO:

Debt ratio = (Total Debt / Total Assets) x 100
$$= (238900 / 716000) \times 100$$
$$= 33.37\%$$

Simply:

The organization's debt equates to one-third of its asset value[2,12].

TIMES INTEREST EARNED:

Time interest earned = Earnings before interest and tax / Interest due
= 98300 / 12000
= 8.19

Simply:

Net profit is able to cover interest due 8.19 times, there for indicating that the organization is still in a positive and stable financial balance[2].

Cost Analysis

Cost Effectiveness and Cost Efficiency

Cost Effectiveness: Includes the number of items produced or goals achieved on time and of acceptable quality[2]. Cost effectiveness further compares the cost and health effects of an intervention to assess the extent to which it can be regarded as providing value for money[16].

Cost Efficiency: Cost efficiency is a measure of the organization's ability to have reached a specified target or goal with the minimum expenditure of resources. Thus the speed of delivering the product or service[2,16]. Cost efficiency is sometimes referred to as the extent to which the program has converted or is expected to convert its resources economically into results in order to achieve the maximum possible outputs, outcomes, and impacts with the minimum possible inputs[15].

> **Simply:**
>
> Cost effectiveness; relates to achieving goals on time and within budget.
>
> Cost efficiency; relates to reaching targets below budget or sooner than proposed timelines. Maximum output with the minimum possible inputs.

COST-BENEFIT ANALYSIS

Cost-benefit analysis is done to establish how well or poorly a planned action will turn out[18] and is the sound financial decision-making analysis of the total cost, versus the total benefit[2].

The cost-benefit analysis finds, quantifies and adds all the positive factors, and then identifies, quantifies and subtracts all the negative factors, costs[18]. The difference between the two indicates whether the planned action is effective and efficient.

Only measuring the effectiveness of a project by its outcomes or outputs is problematic, and would be based on potentially problematic assumption. Therefore, cost-benefit analysis takes the benefits arising from the activities and programs and asks whether these could have been produced at a lower cost compared with alternatives[15].

The cost of benefit will relate to the Value-Of-Money concept, which assesses if the maximum benefit was or can be produced from the resources and costs available.

> **Simply:**
> Cost benefit analysis; attempts to establish the optimal benefit which can be achieved through a given plan of action. The timeline of the given actions and the time value of money has relevance to the cost benefit.

Failure Factors

Internal Failures:

1. No planning and poor management could result in the uncontrolled spending of company resources[2].

2. Lack of cash flow or capital, result in shortcuts being taken and results in difficulty for the company to survive[19].

3. Lack of financial management skills can result in organizations making poor financial decisions which can lead to the failure of the company[2].

4. Corruption and theft can result in the organization being progressively drained of its profits, and inevitably resulting in failure[2].

5. Incremental Budgeting does not involve in-depth analysis of the previous financial records and statements, and only increments of the previous budget are used, possibly losing sight of the actual financial position that the organization finds itself in[2].

External Failures:

1. Macroeconomic policy – deficit reduction, resulting in higher tax spends and interest rates[2].

2. General Economy, Weakness in the economy, especially in specific markets would result in financial risk[20].

3. External Funding dependency put any of the external sources financial risk directly on the recipient company[2].

4. Legal Risks, changes in tax and company regulations, could eat into small businesses profit margins[20].

5. Receivables, if a major client closes its doors, or refuses to pay, this could have a detrimental impact on a small business's operating cash flow and could result in an operational standstill.

Simply:

In an organization, there are various failure factors which could affect the financial operations of the organization. Internal failure factors which can be planned for and addressed by the financial managers, and External failure factors which are beyond the control of the organization and occur mostly in the Macroeconomic environment, which fall under the PESTLE analysis framework.

Formulations, Valuations, and Calculations

The following sections will apply some of the theories explained in the first half of this book. In many cases, it has been found that the theory is easier to understand than to apply, especially when applying them to real world scenarios.

Valuation

Current Value of debentures

JEST Limited is a rapidly growing company and is listed on the stock exchange in 2000. In 2000, the company issued a tranche of 10 000, 10-year debentures with a par value of 1,000 each. The coupon on the debentures is 12% and is paid annually. If the current yield to maturity (YTM) on similar debentures is 14%, the current value of each debenture is:

The value of debentures is derived from the **future value** that it is perceived to carry, which is based on its expected yield to maturity.

Present Value Interest Rate Factor of Annuity(PVIFA)

$$PVIFA_{i\%, n} := \sum_{t=1}^{n} \frac{1}{(1+i)^t}$$

$$PVIF_{i\%, n} := \frac{1}{(1+i)^n}$$

$$Vd = \left(I \times PVIFA_{i\%, n} \right) + \left(M \times PVIF_{i\%, n} \right)$$

$$V_d = \left(I \times \sum_{k=1}^{n} \frac{1}{(1+k)^t} \right) + \left(M \times \frac{1}{(1+k)^n} \right)$$

$$V_d = \left(120 \times \sum_{t=1}^{10} \frac{1}{(1+0.14)^t} \right) + \left(1000 \times \frac{1}{(1+0.14)^{10}} \right)$$

$V_d = (120 \times 5.216) + 269.74$
$V_d = 625.92 + 269.74$
$V_d = 895.66$

Based on the above calculation, the current value of each debenture/bond is 895.66

Simply:

Using the **Present Value Interest Rate Factor of Annuity (PVIFA)** formula, the current value of a debenture based on its various criteria's can be calculated as in the previous paragraph. Paying more than the calculated value results in a premium paid, and likewise, paying less than the calculated value results in a discount.

VALUATION OF PREFERENCE SHARES

Additionally, JEST Limited issued 400 000, 9% preference shares with a par value of 50. The preference shareholders require a return of 12.5%, The current value of each of the preference shares is:

$$PVA_{9\%,\infty} = PVIFA_{9\%,\infty} \times PMT$$

$$PVA_{9\%,\infty} = \frac{1}{0.125} \times 4.5$$

$$PVA_{9\%,\infty} = \frac{1}{0.125} \times 4.5$$

$$PVA_{9\%,\infty} = 8 \times 4.5$$

$$PVA_{9\%,\infty} = 36$$

Based on the above calculation, current value of each of the preference shares is of R36

Simply:

Using the **Present Value Annuity (PVA)** formula, the current value of a preference share based on its various criteria's can be calculated as in the previous paragraph. Paying more than the calculated value results in a premium paid, and likewise, paying less than the calculated value results in a discount.

VALUATION ORDINARY SHARES WITH A VARIABLE GROWTH RATE.

JEST Limited issued 1 million no-par value ordinary shares and is expected to pay a low dividend of 1 per share. Dividends are expected to grow at 12% per year for the subsequent two years. Thereafter, JEST Limited is expected to sustain an annual dividend growth of 8% indefinitely. If the ordinary shareholders require a return of 15%, The current value of each JEST Limited ordinary share is calculated as follows:

Expected Future Dividends for year 1, 2, and 3 respectively:

$i = 12\% = 0.12$

$D_1 = 1$
$D_2 = D_1 \times (1 + i) = 1 \times 1.12 = 1.12$
$D_3 = D_2 \times (1 + i) = 1.12 \times 1.12 = 1.2544$

Present value of expected dividends:

$k = 15\% = 0.15$

$PV_{D1} = D_1/(1+k) = 1/1.15 = 0.8695$
$PV_{D2} = D_2/(1+k) = 1.12/1.15 = 0.9739$
$PV_{D3} = D_3/(1+k) = 1.2544/1.15 = 1.0908$
∴ $PV_{(D1+D2+D3)} = 2.9342$

Present value of ordinary share on Period₃ using Dividend at D₄:

$$D_4 = D_3 \times (1 + i) = 1.2544 \times 1.08 = \mathit{1.354752}$$

Future share value: (Gordon Model of constant growth)
$$SV_3 = D_4/(i-g) = 1.354752/(0.15-0.08) = \mathit{19.3536}$$

$$PV_0 = SV_3/(1+i)^t = 19.3536 / (1.15)^3 = \mathit{12.7253}$$

Present value of ordinary share at Period₀:

$$P_0 = PV_{(D1+D2+D3)} + PV_0 = 2.9342 + 12.7253 = \mathit{15.65951}$$

Based on the above calculation, the current value of each ordinary share is 15.66

Simply:

In order to calculate the **present value of ordinary shares** with a **variable dividend growth rate**, a systematic approach needs to be followed.

In the example we follow the following process:

1. Calculate the **dividend values** of the first 3 periods respectively, starting at 1 after the first year and growth of 12% for two years thereafter.

2. Calculate and summarize the **present value** of each of these dividends.

3. Calculate the 4th period's **dividend** using the proposed 8% dividend growth.

4. Use the **Gordon Growth model** formula to calculate the **expected future value** based on the 4th period's dividend, the 15% expected growth, the 8% dividend growth.

5. Calculate a **present value** of the 4th period's future value.

6. The **present value** of the **ordinary share** should reflect the previously calculated present values of future dividends. Calculate the **present value of the ordinary share** as the sum of all the calculated present values.

TOTAL CAPITAL EMPLOYED BY JEST LIMITED

Debentures Capital:
 10,000 x 895.92 = *8,959,200*
Preference Shares Capital:
 400,000 x 36 = *14,400,000*
Ordinary Shares Capital:
 1,000,000 x 15.66 = *15,660,000*

Total Capital Employed by JEST Limited:
 39,019,200

Simply:

Total Capital Employed reflects the capital value of all debentures, preference, and ordinary shares. Effectively reflecting the total capital investments of investors.

BONDS

In order to finance a new project, JEST Limited plans to issue 10 000, 10-year and 15% coupon bonds. Each bond will be issued at a par value of 1000. In order to make the bonds attractive to investors, the company plans to issue the bonds at a discount of 2.5%. The issue will result in flotation costs of 3% being incurred.

JEST Limited Coupon Bonds:
   Before Tax Cost of Bond[4]:
   Par Value (M): 1000
   Discount: 1000 x 2.5% = 25
   Flotation Cost: 1000 x 3% = 30
   Interest Rate (i): 15%
   Years to Maturity: 10
   Current Value (DB_0): 1000 – 25 – 30 = 945

YIELD TO MATURITY / COST OF BOND

$$YTM = \frac{i + \dfrac{M - DB_0}{n}}{\dfrac{M + DB_0}{2}}$$

$$YTM = \frac{(1000 \times 0.15) + \dfrac{1000 - 945}{10}}{\dfrac{1000 + 945}{2}}$$

$$YTM = \frac{150 + 5.5}{972.5}$$

$$YTM = 0.1598$$

Simply:

Bonds and Debentures are technically the same things and relate to investors loaning an organization a set amount of money with a legal obligation from the company to pay back the money as well as the prescribed interest.

In the example above, the yield to maturity refers to the total rate of return to be received by the investor on the date of the bond maturity. This seems like a simple equation of adding all future interest gains, however since these bonds are being offered at a discounted rate, the YTM should include the capital gains.

From the company's perspective, the YTM relates to the Cost of the bond, however, for the company to accurately calculate the cost include to float the bonds

The above formula is the approximate yield formula, but since we as working with initial listing values, this value can be assumed as the exact yield.

JEST Limited before tax approximate YTM = 16%

AFTER TAX COST OF BOND:

Since costs on debt are tax deductible, the true cost of the bonds can be identified. For the sake of this case, we assume that JEST Limited is taxed annually at 30%.

Tax = 30%

$k_i = k_d(1-\text{Tax})$
$k_i = 15.98(1 - 0.3)$
$k_i = 15.98 \times 0.7$
$k_i = 11.186\%$

Simply:

In most countries, the costs paid on debt is tax deductible, thus the true cost of the bonds can be reduced by the tax value that was benefited.
Cost After Tax = Cost x (1 − Tax)
= 15.98 x 0.7
= 11.186

JEST Limited has an after tax Cost of Bond of 11.186%

COST OF ORDINARY SHARES USING GORDON'S GROWTH MODEL:

At JEST Limited, funds will be raised through the issue of 500 000 ordinary shares at a price of 100 per share. Flotation costs on the new shares are expected to be 2.50 per share. JEST Limited has just paid a dividend of 5 per share on its existing ordinary shares. Dividends on ordinary shares are expected to grow at 10% per annum into the foreseeable future. Using Gordon's dividend growth model, the cost of the ordinary shares can be calculated

Initial value of share (P_0): 100 -2.50
Flotation Cost: 2.50
Current dividend (D_0): 5
Next expected dividend (D_1): $D_0(1+g)$
Constant dividend growth rate (g): 10% = 0.1

Rate of return (k_s):

$$P_0 = \frac{D_1}{k_s - g}$$

$$\therefore k_s = \frac{D_0(1+g)}{P_0} + g$$

$$k_s = \frac{5(1+0.1)}{(100-2.5)} + 0.1$$

$$k_s = \frac{5.5}{97.5} + 0.1$$

$$k_s = 0.564 + 0.1$$

$$k_s = 0.1564$$

Simply:
Since the proposed dividend growth is constant, the Gordons growth model formula can be used to establish the cost of the ordinary shares. In the above example, the equation is rearranged for *Rate of Return* to become the subject of the equation.

Rate of Return = (Next dividend / Net proceeds) + Growth Factor
= (5/97.5) + 0.1
= 0.1564

The cost of ordinary shares is 15.64%

COST OF PREFERENCE SHARES:

JEST Limited plans to issue 100 000, 12% preference shares with a par value of 50 per share. Flotation costs on the preference shares are expected to amount to 2.50 per share. Using the information given above, the cost of JEST Limited's preference shares can be calculated as follows:

Dividend per share (D_p): 50
Cost of floatation (C_f): 2.50
Net proceeds of share sale (Np): P_p - C_f
Cost per share (k_s):

$$k_p = \frac{D_p}{N_p}$$

$$k_p = \frac{D_p}{P_p - C_f}$$

$$k_p = \frac{6}{50 - 2.5}$$

$$k_p = \frac{6}{47.5}$$

$$k_p = 0.1263$$

Simply:

The cost of an ordinary share calculation is as simple as dividing the dividend over the net proceeds, thus deriving the net cost percentage.

= 6/47.5
= 0.1263

The cost of the preference shares is 12.63%

LIMITED WEIGHTED AVERAGE COST OF CAPITAL (WACC): (USING MARKET VALUES AS WEIGHTS)

Market Value and Weight:
  Debt: 10,000 x 1000 = 10,000,000
    .:15.38% of market value
  Ordinary Shares: (500,000 x 100) = 50,000,000
    .:76.92% of market value
  Preference Shares + (100,000 x 50) = 5,000,000
    .:7.7% of market value

Source	Pre-Tax cost	After-Tax cost	Weight	Weighted cost
Debt/Bonds	15.98%	11.186%	15.38%	1.7204%
Ordinary Shares	15.64%	15.64%	76.92%	12.0302%
Preference Shares	12.63%	12.63%	7.7%	0.9725%
WACC				14.7231%

Simply:

Using all the criteria of the previous calculations, we are able to derive the Weighted Average Cost of all the investor capital based on the weight of each type of investment and their market value in relation to the total market value

10mil + 50mil + 5mil = 65mil total value

Cost Comparison Analysis

Cost of In-House versus Outsourcing

JEST Limited is deciding whether to provide catering in-house or to outsource meals. The company's cost of capital is 12%

Using the Present Value Interest Rate factors (PVIF) we can calculate the WACC discount factor for each period, and derive a comparatively accurate cost analysis.

WACC Cost of Capital (i): 12%

Period (n):

$$PVIF_{i\%, n} := \frac{1}{(1+i)^n}$$

Cost of providing Catering in-house:

	Year 0	Year 1	Year 2	Year 3
Kitchen equipment	150,000	-		+75,000
Ingredients		100,000	112,000	-124,000
Salaries of kitchen staff		-40,000	-45,000	-50,000
Opportunity cost of kitchen space		-60,000	-72,000	
Electricity and water		-15,000	-20,000	-25,000
Total in-house costs	150,000	215,000	249,000	-124,000
WACC Discount Factor	1	0.893	0.797	0.712
Discounted Cash flow	-150,00	191,995	198,453	-88,288
NPV				628,736

Cost of outsourcing:

	Year 1	Year 2	Year 3	Year 4
Total outsource	0	-300,000	-350,000	-375,000
WACC Discount Factor	1	0.893	0.797	0.712
Discounted Cash flow	-0	-267,900	-278,950	-267,000
NPV				-813,850

Based on the above calculations, JEST Limited should choose to provide in-house catering as the net present value over a 4-year period indicate that it is 185,114 more cost effective to provide catering in-house.

Simply:

In order for JEST to accurately calculate its cost, each year's total costs need to be translated into a present value based on the company's WACC, this is achieved by making use of the PVIF formula since there in a static interest factor and no annuity factor.

VEHICLE REPLACEMENT ANALYSIS

JEST Limited wants to establish the optimal time for the renewal of their fleet of ten vehicles. The company has three options: renew their fleet in three years, four years or five years. The company's cost of capital is 15%. The costs of renewing and running the fleet are given below.

Three-year option:

	Invest	Cost	Residual	Net Cash Flow	CoC	PVIF	NPV
0	-2,500,000	0	0	-2,500,000	15%	1,000	-2,500,000
1		-200,000		-200,000	15%	0.870	-173,913.04
2		-280,000		-280,000	15%	0.756	-211,720.23
3		-350,000	850,000	500,000	15%	0.658	328 758.12
NPV							-2,556,875.15

Four-year option:

	Invest	Cost	Residual	Net Cash Flow	CoC	PVIF	NPV
0	-2,500,000	0	0	-2,500,000	15%	1,000	-2,500,000
1		-200,000		-200,000	15%	0.870	-173,913.04
2		-280,000		-280,000	15%	0.756	-211,720.23
3		-350,000		-350,000	15%	0.658	-230,130.68
4		-410,000	660,000	250,000	15%	0.572	142,938.31
NPV							-2,972,825.64

Five-year option:

	Invest	Cost	Residual	Net Cash Flow	CoC	PVIF	NPV
0	-2,500,000	0	0	-2,500,000	15%	1.000	-2,500,000
1		-200,000		-200,000	15%	0.870	-173,913.04
2		-280,000		-280,000	15%	0.756	-211,720.23
3		-350,000		-350,000	15%	0.658	-230,130.68
4		-410,000		-410,000	15%	0.572	-234,418.83
5		-500,000	450,000	-50,000	15%	0.497	-24,858.84
NPV							-3,375,041.62

Average Annualized cost of each option:

$<AC_3> = NPV / 3$
$<AC_3> = 2556875.15 / 3$
$<AC_3> = 852291.72$

$<AC_4> = NPV / 4$
$<AC_4> = 2972825.64 / 4$
$<AC_4> = 743206.41$

$<AC_5> = NPV / 5$
$<AC_5> = 3375041.62 / 5$
$<AC_5> = 843760.41$

Annualized equivalent cost of each option:

$AC_3 = NPV / PVIFA_{15\%, 3}$
$AC_3 = 2556875.15 / 2.283$
$AC_3 = 1119962.83$

$AC_4 = NPV / PVIFA_{15\%, 4}$
$AC_4 = 2972825.64 / 2.855$
$AC_4 = 1041269.93$

$AC_5 = NPV / PVIFA_{15\%, 5}$
$AC_5 = 3375041.62 / 3.352$
$AC_5 = 1006873.99$

Based on the above calculations, the optimal renewal period for JEST Limited's fleet is 5 years.

Simply:

To compare the cost of asset based on its annualized costs, the same formula (PVIF) as in the previous example is used to totaled together to arrive at the total Net Present Value (NPV). However, given the net present value, one can simply derive an average annualized cost by simply dividing by the periods. Because this produces only averages, does not accurately take into account the compound nature of interest, one needs to divide the NPV with the PFIFA factor for the given period, and the given interest(cost) to establish the most accurate annualized cost.

This becomes clear when comparing the results of the average annualized cost versus the annualized equivalent cost.

Organization Valuation

Relevance of Dividend on the Value of a Firm

Relevance of Dividend on the value of a firm; relevant theory with empirical examples;

There are generally two schools of thought with regards to dividend policy[21], Firstly, the irrelevance theory and secondly the relevance theory, both contradicting each other, and both without satisfactory guidelines, and with these contradictions effectively leading to a dividend controversy.

Neither the price of a firm's stocks nor the cost of capital are affected by its dividend policy[22]. However, this theory is based on a couple of critical assumptions as follows:

1. Involves no personal or corporate taxes.
2. Involves no stock flotation cost or transaction costs.
3. No influence of financial leverage on cost of capital.
4. Full transparency of the firm's future prospects.
5. No effect on the cost of equity based on dividend and retained income split.
6. Dividend policy has zero effect on firm's capital budgeting.

These assumptions are unrealistic to reality circumstances where both commercial and personal income taxes have to be paid. Flotation cost, as well as transaction and trading cost, are often significant. A firm's cost of capital can be affected by dividend policy based on taxation as well as transaction costs. Investors hardly ever have access to the same information as firm's managers. This irrelevance theory is less relevant to smaller investors as the ratio of the costs have a greater impact based on their trading volumes[4].

According to Myron Gordon's Gordon Growth Model[28] there exists a direct correlation between the dividend policy and the value of shares[23]. Additionally, the value that an investor pays for the shares he purchased is based on one of three hypotheses; One; both dividends and earnings, Two; only dividends and Three; only earnings. Gordon's model states that an investor buys a share with the future value in mind and that that future value is directly related to the expected dividends and earnings on the purchase date since the dividend directly correlates to the payment stream that the investor will receive. Thus, stock prices should bear a direct relation to earnings and dividends.

Why do corporations pay dividends, and why do investors pay attention to dividends can be answered? If a firm does not pay dividends, but invests the retained earnings in capital investments which in turn may result in higher capital appreciation and less tax than the dividend pay-outs[24]. This, in turn, could result in a higher stock value. However, in some cases, capital gains are taxed higher than dividends, but this occurrence does not have enough impact to balance the gained effect. Thus with the involvement of tax, from either perspective, investors are indifferent to the level of dividends.

In an attempt to identify whether dividends result in a reaction in the stock price, Ali & Chowdhury[21] in 2010, in an empirical study of the reaction of stock prices to the announcement of the dividends of the banking industry of Bangladesh, found that out of the 25 stocks that they monitored. 11 stocks indicated declines, 6 indicated raises and the remaining 8 showed no change. Ali & Chowdhury showed that a strong contribution to the effect of the stock price can be attributed to possible insider trading as well as other influencing factors and that the results of their statistically pooled test indicated that the stock price reaction to dividends was not statistically significant enough to derive a distinct conclusion.

Numerous such empirical studies have been carried out to determine the stock market reaction to dividend announcements. In 1974, Black and Scholes[45], showed that an increase in the dividend payout might result in a temporary response in the stock price, however, will have no definite effect on the price. In 2005, Docking, Scott, Koch and Poul[46], showed that when the announcements of dividends changes go against the grain of the anticipated change, it elicited significant impact on the price of stocks.

Simply:
Various research studies similar to the ones cited here have concluded that there are too many perspectives and subjective perceptions that play a role in the value of stocks. These studies highlighted that the **dividend relevance / irrelevance theory** is truly a **dividend controversy** based on an array of variables.

SHARE VALUE MANIPULATION PRIOR TO SHARE BUYBACK.

Both post-buyback, as well as reported improvement in performance, are at least partially driven by pre-buyback downward earning management as opposed to genuine profitability[25]. The increase in downward earnings management has a direct relation to the percentage of the buyback as well as the CEO ownership. The downward earnings are generally managed by means of abnormally large pre-buyback accruals which decrease this income of the firm. This, in turn, results in decreased expectations for post-buyback returns, which further drives the post-purchase growth.

In a recent mass buyback of apple shares[26], announced on February 7, 2014, the pre-buyback trend is evident as Apple shares fell eight percent one day after the company reported lower-than-expected holiday-period iPhone sales and issued a weak revenue forecast on January 27, 2014.

In further research of the results and SENS of 25 companies on RTT News, 2014[27], 2 firms showed evidence of similar patterns as to described above:

Unum (UNM) – NYSE:

04 November 2013	Decline in profits for Q3 even though the expectations were for stable profits.
13 December 2013	$750 mil stock buyback announced
16 December 2013 – 9 January 2014	Profit estimates are increased continuously

Fairchild Semiconductor Inter (FCS) – Nasdaq

17 October 2013	Declares profit down for Q3
12 December 2013	$100 mil stock buyback announced
23 January 2014	Profit up for Q4

However, even though the above two firms indicate the suspected patterns as described before, by no means is this conclusive evidence that these firm's share values were manipulated by the managers.

> **Simply:**
>
> Various results have indicated that in some cases of share buyback, a possible manipulation may have taken place. In the examples used, a clear pattern can be derived:
> 1. Low profits or weak revenue forecast results share price drop.
> 2. Stock buyback announced
> 3. Profit increase is announced for the subsequent period
>
> This, however, is not conclusive evidence of intentional price-fixing.

Financial Management in Practice

The purpose of this section is to explore deeper into the fundamentals of finance management both domestically and internationally, demonstrating and applying some of the concepts and practices pertaining to various areas such as ratio analysis, finance, capital management, mergers, and acquisitions as well as forwards markets. In this sections, case studies will be used as examples to illustrate and explain the use of these theories as had been detailed in the previous two sections.

Ratio Analysis

This section deals with ratio analysis and demonstrates calculation on how the different ratio analysis formulas can portray different perspective of an organization's current financial position as well as potential future position and investment opportunity. Additionally, demonstrates how a comparative analysis of these ratios can be used to compare organizations' current performance against each other. It is, however, important to note that organizations within the same market are more accurately comparable since they may operate under similar circumstances.

CALCULATIONS

According to the financial statements for the past three years of two similar companies listed on the Johannesburg Stock Exchange (JSE). The calculated profitability, liquidity and solvency ratios of the two companies are as follows:

	Impala Platinum Holdings Ltd (IMPJ)				African Rainbow Minerals Ltd (ARIJ)			
	2013	2012	2011	3YA	2013	2012	2011	3YA
Net Profit Margin	3.58%	15.58%	20.55%	13.24%	8.69%	19.68%	23.18%	17.18%
Gross Profit Margin	16.82%	22.67%	35.14%	24.88%	36.05%	36.82%	42.21%	38.36%
ROI	1.33%	5.92%	10.07%	5.77%	4.67%	10.11%	10.99%	8.59%
ROE	3.04%	12.30%	19.95%	11.76%	9.24%	19.12%	22.03%	16.79%
Current Ratio	2.79	2.25	2.27	2.44	2.82	2.40	2.41	2.54
Quick Ratio	1.44	1.09	1.43	1.32	2.10	1.79	1.83	1.91
Total Debt Ratio	32.34%	27.75%	26.62%	28.90%	33.20%	30.90%	31.54%	31.88%
Debt-equity	20.51%	8.25%	4.97%	11.24%	17.07%	11.86%	14.46%	14.46%
Times Interest Earned	5.25	18.33	19.23	14.27	14.92	22.48	25.00	20.80

FINDINGS AND MOTIVATION

According to the above ratio analysis, African Rainbow Minerals Ltd (ARIJ) offer the most promising investment potential between the two options based on prior and current performance. Both organizations indicate declined profits, yet both posted increased revenues. The decline in earning is attributed to the continuing decline in US dollar commodity prices on the global market. The industry was further negatively impacted by increased labor unrest in South Africa[29]. Analyzing the above-calculated ratios reflects and supports these findings as follows:

For the sake of a more balanced result, a 3-year average was calculated for each ratio across both organizations.

1. Net profit margin indicates that on average ARIJ is almost 5% more profitable than Impala Platinum Holdings Ltd (IMPJ), which results in higher earnings per share[30]. Net profit indicates the amount of profit the firm has earned for each R1 in revenue[23]. Both firms, however, have indicated a sharp drop in net profits for the 2013 financial year, with drops in net profit margins of 50% and 75% respectively. Indicating a possible increase in the cost of sales and operations expenses across the industry.

2. Gross profit margins of ARIJ were stable across the three years, this was primarily driven by increased sales volumes[29], whereas IMPJ indicated a sharp drop in gross profit margin for 2013. Gross profit margin indicates the profit the firm makes in terms of its cost of sales[23]. Both the Net profit margin, as well as the Gross profit margin, are subjective to the production or operational strategy that the firm follows and do not solely indicate the firm's viability.

3. Return on investment (ROI) for IMPJ further indicates a strong decrease over the last 3 years with a year on year decrease of +/- 4%, indicating that the firm's effectiveness in generating profits with available assets is on the decline. ARIJ show a stable ROI across 2011 and 2012 with a +/- 5% decline in 2013, There is a notable relationship between ROI and Net profit margin, the higher/lower the Net profit margin, the higher/lower the ROI respectively[23].

4. Return on Investors Equity (ROE) for IMPJ, show a similar year on year decline, whereas ARIJ indicates a less accelerated decline. The ROE indicated the profit the companies earned from the investment its shareholders made either via retained earnings or direct investment via shares or bonds.

5. Current ratios for both firms are similar and indicate that both firms have on average 2.5 times the capacity to pay for their current liabilities with their current assets[23].

6. Quick ratios for ARIJ indicate that it is in a more favorable position to settle current liabilities with current assets that are faster to convert to cash than inventory. Since inventory takes longer to convert to cash than any other asset it is excluded from the current assets for the sake of this calculation[30].

7. Total Debt ratios for both firms indicate that on average 30% of both firm assets are financed by creditors.

8. Debt Equity ratios for both firms indicate an increase in borrowing for both organizations for 2013, IMPJ with a 150% increase in funds provided by creditors other than the firm's owners, whereas ARIJ's creditor funding only increased by 45%. This ratio indicates that IMPJ is financially leveraged to a much higher degree than ARIJ, this could indicate that both firms are attempting to seek more profits with borrowed fund[30].

9. Times interest earned for ARIJ, indicate that the firm has the ability to pay the interest on its borrowing in excess of 14 times, whereas IMPJ has the ability to pay the interest on its borrowing +/- 5 times. This indicates that ARIJ can significantly afford further debt more than IMPJ, however, a figure of 5 and above is regarded as an acceptable figure[23].

Simply:

In the various subsections of this analysis, it becomes clear that not any one single method of comparative analysis is sufficient to analyze the performance of organizations. Thus, it is imperative to use a combination of methods to establish a good candidate for investment.

Effective Cost of Factoring

Case Study

JEST Limited is a fast-growing manufacturer of automotive parts. The company is in dire need of cash and is considering factoring its accounts receivables (debtors). Its sales are 40 million per annum, all on credit. It has been offered the following terms by a factor:

- Seventy-five percent of each invoice could be drawn by JEST Limited immediately on presentation.

- Interest will be charged at 1% above prime (assume a prime of 15.5%).

- The service fee will be 1.5% of sales.

- JEST Limited's average collection period is 60 days.

If the company factors its receivables, it would be able to pay its suppliers in time to take a 3.5% cash settlement discount.

JEST Limited's annual purchases which are subject to a settlement discount are 45% of sales. In addition, the use of full factoring is expected to save the firm part of one employee's salary of 60,000 per annum.

(The employee can be re-deployed to another department to avoid the cost of a new hire in that department.). Telephone, stationery and other incidental costs saved are expected to amount to 5,000 per annum.

The effective cost of factoring will be:
Annual sales – 40,000,000
Factorable – 75%
Interest - 16.5% per annum
Service fee – 1.5% of sales
Average collection period = 60 Days
Supplier early settle discount = 3.5%
45% of annual sales subject to supplier discount
Savings on fixed costs = (Part of 60,000)
Savings on incidental costs = 5,000

Since JEST Limited can factor only 75% of sales and average collection period is 60 days, the average amount to be factored will be 75% of 60 days' sales.

Average maximum amount factored:

∴ 0.75 x ((60/365) x 40,000,000.00) = 4,931,506.849

The assumption is that the service fee is applicable to the total annual sales figure.

Factoring costs:
Est interest per annum:

0.165 x 4,931,506.849 = 813,698.6301

Est service fee per annum:

= 0.015 x 40,000,000.00
= 600,000.00

∴ Total estimated factor costs:

= 813,698.6301 + 600,000.00
= 1,413,698.63

Pre Savings Cost of factoring:

= 1,413,698.63 / 4,931,506.849
= 0.28666
= 28.67%

Factoring savings:
Annual Supplier Discount:

= 0.035 x 0.45 x 40,000,000.00
= 630,000

Internal Cost Savings:

= 60,000.00 + 5,000.00
= 65,000.00

.: Total Cost Savings:
= 695,000.00

.: Net Cost of Factoring:

= 1,413,698.63 – 695,000.00
= 718,698.63

.: The Effective Cost of Factoring:

= 718,698.63 / 4,931,506.849
= 0.14573
= 14.57 %

By virtue of the above savings directly resulting from the factoring, the effective cost of factoring is 14.57% and is a reduction of almost half of pre-savings cost of the factoring of 28.67%.

Simply:

This section deals with cost factoring and demonstrates how to determine the effective costs of factoring when offsetting the factor costs with the early settlement discounts of the supplier. This case study demonstrates, that in some cases it is more cost-effective to make use of factoring to ensure improved net results and production.

Summary of calculations:

Costs of Factoring: *1,413,698.63*

Saving as result of Factoring: *695,000.00*

.: Net Cost of Factoring: *718,698.63*

Which equates to 14.6% effective cost of factoring, which is less than the given interest rate, thus less than the possible cost of taking on trade loans.

CAPITAL STRUCTURE DETERMINING APPROACHES

The three basic approaches to determining optimal ratios between short-term and long-term financing are as follows[30]:

Aggressive financing approach; to financing offers high risk as well as high profitability; When the aggressive approach is used, firms will finance all of its temporary assets as well as some of its permanent assets with short-term, nonspontaneous debt and financing fixed assets with long-term capital[31]. This approach is sometimes referred to as "Relatively Aggressive"[32], as there can be different levels of aggressiveness for example having all permanent current assets as well as some fixed assets financed with short-term credit, would be regarded as a highly aggressive, extremely non-conservative approach and subject a firm to high volatility with regards to rising interest rates. However, short-term debt is often cheaper than long-term debt and firms pushing for higher profits by adopting this approach potentially sacrifice capital safety[32]. Firms adopting an aggressive approach may further benefit from any declines in short-term rates[33].

Moderate or Maturity matching approach (hedging); requires that a firm should attempt to exactly match the maturities of assets and liabilities. This is the most optimal approach to financing as it offers moderate risk as well as moderate profitability, and enables the firm to reach a balance between liquidity and cost of idle funds[31]. Because of the precise management of asset maturities and liabilities, a balance is achieved between lower interest costs and loss of profitability. The risk of bankruptcy is limited to extreme situations. This approach is, however, further complicated by uncertainties in the life of an asset. With this approach, firms should finance inventory, equipment, and capital assets with loans of similar terms than that of the items time to sell, economic or useful life[32].

Conservative financing approach; to financing offers low risk as well as low profitability[31]. When adopting the conservative approach, firms choose to use long term capital to finance permanent assets as well as catering for some of their seasonal financial needs[34]. In this approach, firms only use short-term credit to finance its requirements during temporary periods. It is important to note that when a firm that is adopting a conservative approach has a low need for temporary current assets, that its long-term financing will exceed its total assets, which will allow firms to invest excess funds into marketable securities[33].

Several factors play a role when companies choose an approach to working capital structures, lack of access to capital markets could be a reason for a firm to choose a conservative approach. Whereas a potential of interest rates falling could temps firms to adopt a more aggressive approach. However, firms who wish to concentrate on value maximization could follow a maturity-matching approach by hedging against interest rate changes[33].

> **Simply:**
>
> This section discusses the three most common capital structure determining approaches and details the differences between aggressive, moderate and conservative approaches
>
> **Aggressive**: Finance short, and long term assets
>
> **Moderate**: Finance, some of the assets, and attempt to match maturities of assets with the liabilities.
>
> **Conservative**: Finance mostly long term assets, and short-term finance only in times of need.

OPERATING AND CASH CONVERSION CYCLE

JEST Limited is a t-shirt shop and buys and sells trendy and exclusive t-shirts to socialites in high profile centers and other areas. The organization is experiencing working capital problems and has to resolve the problems. JEST Limited's financials show that the shop takes 45 days to sell its inventory, 90 days to collect cash from its customers (most of the customers buy on credit), and 30 days to pay its suppliers.

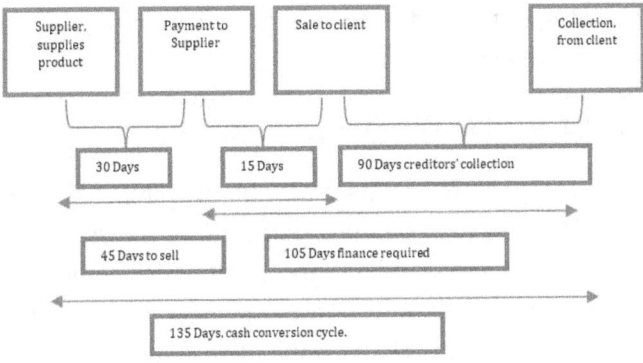

Critical assumptions:
1. Payment period starts on the day of delivery from supplier.
2. Age of inventory starts on the day of delivery from supplier.
3. Collection period starts on day of sale to client

Calculation:
- 30 average days for payment (APP) to the supplier from the date of delivery.
- 45 average days' age of inventory (AAI) from the date of delivery.
- 90 days to collect cash from the customer (ACP) from the day of sale.

.: Operating cycle(OC) = AAI + ACP = 135 days
.: Cash Conversion Cycle(CCC) = AAI + ACP - APP = 105 days

Based on the above calculations, JEST Limited has an operating cycle of 135 days which currently has a positive cash conversion cycle of 105 days. This causes a cash flow deficit and requires that JEST acquires possible unsecured short-term finance to support the cash conversion cycle[30].

STRATEGIES TO IMPROVE CASH CONVERSION CYCLE

There are various strategies to minimize a positive cash conversion cycle, however, firms should take care not to use these strategies to the disadvantage of the organization. Three of these strategies are as follows:

Stretching account payable

A firm can stretch its accounts payable by paying bills as late as possible, however, this has ethical implications and could lead to a violation of supplier agreement which could result in refusal for future credit. Additionally, this could result in the firm missing out on early settlement discounts which could turn out to be more profitable than the benefit of stretching payables and potentially risking late payment penalties.

Efficient purchasing and inventory management

A firm could improve its cash conversion cycles by improving its inventory turnover. By improving forecasting and demand management techniques, firms can execute higher levels of control on inventory and contribute to more efficient inventory turnover as well as a reduced inventory purchasing cycle. Due to this approach being more scientific, it would require higher levels of involvement and control.

Speeding up the collection of accounts receivable

Speeding up the collection of accounts receivable is another way that a firm can improve on its cash conversion cycle as accounts receivable ties up cash which could be invested more profitably into other assets. However, the actual credit terms could be dictated by the industry of firm. Firms in industries with highly diversified products and services, have less risk of differentiated collection times negatively impacting on its market share, whereas firms in industries that have limited differentiation in products and services derive part of their competitive edge from their collection strategy.

> **Simply:**
>
> This section demonstrates how an organization's cash conversion cycle can be determined, and further discusses what organizations can do to improve their cash conversion cycles.
>
> Cash conversions cycles can be improved either by increasing payment cycles, which could lead to bad credit and penalties, JIT inventory management, which would require hands-on involvement and monthly analytics; Shorter collection cycles, however, this could lead to loss of potential customers.

Cost of Inventory and Capital Management

JEST Limited specializes in buying and selling t-shirts of different colors. The company currently orders 250 t-shirts per week. Each t-shirt costs 100. T-Shirts ordered are usually sold out by the end of the week. The carrying cost per t-shirt is 25 per year and the fixed cost per order is 200.

The total carrying cost:
1 x 250 units order per week
250 units' average sold per week
100 per unit cost
Annual per unit carry cost: 25
Fixed cost per order(F): 200
52 weeks per year

Annual units sold (S):
= 250 x 52
= 13000

Annual fixed cost:
= 200 x 52
= 10,400

Average in inventory on hand:
= (Inventory
= ((13000)/52)/2
= 250/2
= 125 unit average in inventory on hand.

Total carrying\storing costs (TCC):
= Average Inventory x Carry cost per unit
= 125 x 25
= 3,125 total cost of carrying inventory

Restocking\Ordering cost (TOC):
= Fixed costs per order x Total orders per year
= *100 x 52*
= *5,200 restocking cost*

Carry cost as % of inventory:
= Carry cost / Average inventory x 100
= *25 / 13000 x 100*
= *0.1923%*

.: Economic Order Quantity(EOQ)[30]:

$$= \sqrt{\frac{2 \times (F \times S)}{C \times P}}$$

$$= \sqrt{\frac{2 \times (200 \times 13{,}000)}{0.1923 \times 100}}$$

$$= \sqrt{\frac{2 \times (2{,}600{,}000)}{19.23}}$$

$$= \sqrt{\frac{5{,}200{,}000}{19.23}}$$

$$= \sqrt{270{,}410.8164}$$

$$= 520.01$$

Number of orders per year required

Increasing the units per order count decreases the frequency of the need to restock, which in turn reduces the number of orders needed per year.

Current Orders per Year = 52 Orders of 250 units
.: Proposed Orders per Year:
= Units sold per year / EOQ
= 13000 / 520
= 25

Simply:

The EOQ equation attempts to establish the optimum order quantity that an organization should carry given the cost of production, demand rate and carry costs.

In these equations, many of the relevant values relating to EOQ is calculated. The EOQ is calculated using the annual inventory as the case study stipulates that usually, all units sell out. In the case study, for JEST Limited to attain the optimal capital management strategy, they should increase their order quantity to 520 units per order.

With this proposed EOQ of 520, JEST Limited will reduce their orders from 52 per year to only 25 per year.

Cost-Volume-Profit

JEST Limited manufactures watches and sells them for 5,000 per unit. The company presently assembles and sells 100,000 units per year. Unit variable manufacturing and selling expenses are 2,500 and 500 respectively. Fixed costs are 50 million for factory overheads and 25 million for selling and administration activities.

Sales Price: *5,000.00* per unit
Units sold per year: *100,000*

Variable Costs per unit:
Manufacture: *2,500.00*
Sales: *500*

Fixed Costs Per:
- Factory: 50m,
- Sales and Admin: 25m

Number of units needed to break even:
Q_{BE} = Fixed Cost / (Profit Contribution)
= Fixed Cost / (Sales Price – Variable Cost)
= *75,000,000 / (5,000 – 3,000)*
= *75,000,000 / 2,000*
= *37,500*

According to the above calculation, JEST Limited needs to sell 37,500 watch units per annum in order to break even.

Number of units to be sold to double up profits and reach 75m operating profit:

Q_{OP} = Target profit contribution / (Unit Profit Contribution)

= Target Profit Contribution / (Sales Price − Variable Cost)
= 75,000,000 / (5,000 − 3,000)
= 75,000,000 / 2,000
= 37,500

Therefore, JEST Limited needs to sell 37,500 additional units above the Q_{BE} quantity, thus Galaxy has to sell 75,000 units to reach R75m operating profit.

Simply:

Cost volume analysis attempts to establish the sales volumes required to achieve specified profit targets. In the case of breakeven analysis, the targeted profits would be set as zero.

The equation to calculate these quantities are as follows:

Target / (Sales Price - Variable cost)

In the case of breakeven analysis, the target can be accepted as the total fixed cost of the organization. In the case of target profits, the target should be set at the sum of fixed cost and target profits.

In the equation, these target quantities are calculated independently and summed together for the total proposed quantity

MERGERS AND ACQUISITIONS

REASON FOR MERGERS AND ACQUISITIONS WITH FOCUS ON THE SOUTH AFRICAN MARKET

The South African Competition Act of 1998 introduced a new competition regime that would significantly change the merger review in South Africa[35].

The South African market is still riddled with high levels of market concentration, resulting in niche market power being protected by concentrated ownerships for several important industries. However, during the last decade of reform, the tight integrations of some of the old South African concentrations started unbundling their focused structures in such companies like Anglo American Corp. This unbundling, as well as international and domestic economic growth in addition to BEE charters and procurement codes, was the most significant drivers of the steady rise of Mergers and Acquisitions between 2001 till 2007. The Competition commission defines a merger as the action of one or more firms directly or indirectly acquiring or establishing direct or indirect control over the whole or part of the business of another firm.

Since 1995, mergers and acquisitions notably increased mainly due to the lifting of international economic sanctions as well as the inclusion of South Africa into the global economic framework[36]. The enhancement of the BEE act in 2003 further accelerated the drastic increase in mergers and acquisitions with a majority of BEE transactions securing between 10 – 25% and 25 – 50% ownership transfer. Of the total mergers and acquisition deals of ZAR284 billion in 2006 and ZAR514 billion in 2007, ZAR56 billion and ZAR96 billion respectively were attributed to BEE empowerment deals that were likely driven by compliance to legislation.

The majority of the large portion of mergers and acquisition transactions between 2003 and 2008 to the mining industry, indicating that these transactions consisted of more than 130 deals spread across coal, platinum and gold mining. However, pre-2009, the manufacturing sector was the biggest drive of mergers and acquisitions and averaged 26% of all mergers, followed by property, wholesale and retail.

This multidimensional boom in mergers and acquisitions reached its peak during 2007/2008 and was highly attributed as the partial result of the liberation and restructuring of the South African economy accompanied with the growth of the global financial markets and private equity activities[35]. However, that the international financial crisis in 2009 led to a drastic drop in mergers and acquisition numbers. Since this 2008/2009 crisis, the majority of the mergers and acquisition deals have involved foreign investors mainly from eastern countries like China, Japan, and India as well as notable investment from the USA, a drastic reduction of BEE deals was a significant difference from the years prior to the financial crisis[37]. This significant growth in the mergers and acquisitions market prior to 2007 was further fueled by a drastically growing South African economy which at that stage had reached a rate of growth in excess of 5% per annum.

In a 2012 Mergers and Acquisitions report[38], investors' appetite in the South African market were gradually being restored and that half of the deals made in Africa for 2012 were focused on South African businesses.

With the coming into effect of the South African Companies Act of 2008 in middle 2011, the mergers and acquisitions arena was significantly impacted especially the regulation regarding takeovers which is largely based on the UK City Code of takeover[40]. Even though in 2011 the mergers and acquisitions activity globally was down by more than 24%[41], South African along with the Middle Eastern markets, were the only markets showing an increase, even though, as a negative perception about South African markets existed amongst investors not yet doing business in the continent. The success of South African-based global equity traders can be attributed to the significant mergers and acquisitions activity in South Africa as a result of South Africa's highly developed BEE policies[41].

Simply:

The aim of this sections is to discuss the last decade of Mergers and Acquisitions in the South African market and discusses in detail some of the critical factors that lead to the rapid increase and high volumes of Mergers and Acquisitions in South Africa.

In conclusion, it is notable that the two major drivers of the South African mergers and acquisitions activities over the past decades can strongly be attributed to the strong BEE activities pairing with a strongly growing economy.

Forward Market

Germany vs South Africa

A forward market is a marketplace to contractually and upfront lock in future financial transactions, trades at a predetermined rate when possible future trading rates could fluctuate and negatively impact on parties in the trade[42,43]. E.g.: currency exchange rates, interest rates, commodities, and securities.

Many studies have found that the forward rate set on the contractual agreement is a fairly bias predictor of the future change in the spot exchange rate[44], however generally in the opposite direction as the actual movement, However, their finding have indicated that this is mostly only applicable to advanced economies and major currencies, and attribute this behavior to the more predictable trends and depreciation of emerging markets.

Simply:

This final section discusses the benefits to using a forward market transaction to minimize the risk of cross-currency transactions.

In the case of an organization using the forward market to lock in a fixed future exchange rate for the purchase of supplies for a period of 60 days, as well as potentially using the market trend to speculate of the potential future movement of the exchange rate enables the organization to establish a more accurate costing budget, as well as protect financial interests if the exchange rate fluctuates.

About The Author

Jan H Pieterse is the founder of *NextCEO*, a member of Mensa, serial entrepreneur, specialist software engineer and the author of various business and information technology related articles. He has authored various other articles under pen names. He lives in Centurion, South Africa with his wife and two sons. With almost two decades of hands-on experience, he is a veteran in the information technology field. Entrepreneurship, business management, and leadership have always been at the forefront of his aspirations. He was a co-founder of various companies and has contributed and consulted on business development and strategic processes of several of organizations.

Learn more about Jan H Pieterse at NextCEO.co.za

OTHER BOOKS BY JAN H PIETERSE

At the time of publishing this edition of the book, I am in process of authoring the below books, please go to my website nextceo.co.za and sign up with your details and I will send you a personal email when they are published:

- The Simple Side of Human Resource Management
- The Simple Side of Financial Management
- The Simple Side of Strategic Management
- The Simple Side of Marketing Management
- The Simple Side of Project Management
- The Simple Side of Economics
- The Simple Side of Negotiation and Conflict Management
- The Simple Side of Information, Communication and Technology Management

You can get all my books on my Author Central page:

Jan H Pieterse http://amzn.to/2esEZOd

One Last Thing

If you enjoyed this book or found it useful I'd be very grateful if you'd post a short review on Amazon. Your support really does make a difference and I read all the reviews personally so I can get your feedback and make this book even better.

If you'd like to leave a review, then all you need to do is click the review link on this book's page on Amazon here:

Review here: http://amzn.to/2dSox8b

Thank you again for your support!

Bibliography

1. Managementstudyguide.com. (2013). Financial Management - Meaning, Objectives and Functions. Retrieved Feb 19, 2013, from http://www.managementstudyguide.com/financial-management.htm

2. Regenesys. (2012). Marketing Management Study Guide, BBA 1. Johannesburg: Regenesys.

3. Investopedia.com. (2013a). Future Value Definition. Retrieved from Investopedia.com, viewed on 30 Jan 2013: http://www.investopedia.com/terms/f/futurevalue.asp

4. Regenesys. (2013). Financial Management II. Johannesburg: Regenesys.

5. Correira, C., Flynn, D., Uliana, E. & Wormald, M. (2007) Financial Management. Cape Town: Juta & Co.

6. Bragg, S. (2010). What is Incremental Budgeting. Retrieved from Accounting tools.com, Viewed on 31 Jan 2013: http://www.accountingtools.com/questions-and-answers/what-is-incremental-budgeting.html

7. Branat, R. (2005). Zero-Base Budgets. Retrieved from 24xls.com, viewed on 31 Jan 2013: http://www.strategic-control.24xls.com/en209

8. Investopedia.com. (2013c). Activity-Based Budgeting. Retrieved from Investopedia.com, viewed on 31 Jan 2013: http://www.investopedia.com/terms/a/abb.asp

9. Finance Doctors. (2011). Standard costing and variance analysis. Retrieved from Finance Doctors, viewed on 31 Jan 2013.

10. Accounting 4 Management. (2013). Usefulness of Variance. Retrieved from Accounting 4 Management, viewed on 31 Jan 2013: http://accounting4management.com/usefulness_of_variances.htm

11. Investopedia.com. (2013d). Financial Ratios Tutorial. Retrieved from Investopedia.com viewed on 13 Feb 2013.

12. Stoltz, A., Viljoen, M., Gool, S., Meyer, C., & Cronje. (2007). Financial Management: Fresh. Cape Town: Pearson Education.

13. Accountingtools.com. (2011). What is days' sales in inventory? Retrieved from Accounting tools - viewed on 07 Feb 2013: http://www.accountingtools.com/questions-and-answers/what-is-days-sales-in-inventory.html

14. Investopedia.com. (2013e). Definition of 'Days Sales Of Inventory - DSI'. Retrieved from Investopedia.com - view on 07 Feb 2013: http://www.investopedia.com/terms/d/dsi.asp

15. World Bank. (2012). Efficiency or Cost-Effectiveness. Retrieved Feb 19, 2013, from http://siteresources.worldbank.org/EXTGLOREGPARPROG/Resources/grpp_source book_chap11.pdf

16. Philips, C., & Thompson, G. (2009). What is Cost-effectiveness. Health economics (1), 8.

17. wiki.answers.com. (2013). Wiki Answers. Retrieved Feb 16, 2013, from http://wiki.answers.com/Q/What_is_difference_between_cost_efficiency_and_cost_effectiveness

18. About.com. (2013). About.com - Management. Retrieved Feb 16, 2013, from http://management.about.com/cs/money/a/CostBenefit.htm

19. Holman, V. (2011). Why businesses fail - Youtube. Retrieved Feb 19, 2013, from http://www.youtube.com/watch?v=wNO-2fq1gqc

20. Chron.com, Ingram, D., & Media, D. (2013). External and Internal Factors of Financial Risk. Retrieved Feb 19, 2013, from http://smallbusiness.chron.com/external-internal-factors-financial-risk-4563.html

21. Ali, M. B., & Chowdhury, T. A. (2010). Effect of Dividend on Stock Price in Emerging Stock Market: A Study. International Journal of Economics and Finance, 52-64.

22. Pilarczyk, M. (2014). Dividend irrelevance theory. Retrieved 02 22, 2014, from Encyclopedia of Management: http://mfiles.pl/en/index.php/Dividend_irrelevance_theory

23. Stoltz, A., Viljoen, M., Gool, S., Meyer, C., & Cronje, R. (2007). Financial Management: Fresh Perspectives. Cape Town: Pearson Education.

24. Black, F. (1976). The Dividend Puzzle. The Journal of Portfolio Management, Vol. 2, No. 2:, 5-8.

25. Gong, G., Louis, H., & Sun, A. (2008). Earnings management and firm performance following open-market repurchase. Journal of Accounting and Economics Vol. 63(2), p. 947-986.

26. Robert Galbraith. (2014, 02 07). Apple buys back $14 billion of shares in two weeks since results. Retrieved 03 01, 2014, from reuters.com: http://www.reuters.com/article/2014/02/07/us-apple-repurchase-idUSBREA1606820140207

27. RTT News. (2014, 02 28). Stock Buyback Announcements. Retrieved 03 02, 2014, from rttnews.com: http://www.rttnews.com/corpinfo/StockBuybacks.aspx

28. Gordon, M. (1959). Dividends, Earnings, and Stock Prices. The Review of Economics and Statistics Vol. 41, No. 2, Part 1, 99-105.

29. Motsepe, P. (2013). Executive Chaiman's report. Retrieved from ARM Reports: http://arm.integrated-report.com/2013/downloads/ARM-IR13-management-review.pdf

30. Marx, J., & Swart, C. d. (2013). Financial Management in South Africa 4ed. Cape Town: Pearson.

31. efinancemanagement.com. (2014, 07 31). Compare 3 Strategies of Working Capital Financing. Retrieved from efinancemanagement: http://www.efinancemanagement.com/working-capital-financing/272-compare-3-strategies-of-working-capital-financing-maturity-matching-hedging-conservative-and-aggressive-approach

32. Scott Besley, E. B. (2008). Essentials of Managerial Finance. http://books.google.co.za/books?id=oi9sOjf4cv8C&pg=PA580&lpg=PA580&dq=Moderate+or+Maturity+matching+approach&source=bl&ots=6GG_SawIAt&sig=bFCDKCpV8a1haLfCofqYXNwFnRw&hl=en&sa=X&ei=65jaU6PFO8Lb0QW_2IDwCQ&ved=0CD4Q6AEwBA#v=onepage&q=Moderate%20or%20Maturity.

33. H. Kent Baker, G. P. (2005). Understanding Financial Management: A Practical Guide. Victoria: Blackwell Publishing Ltd.

34. Eugene Brigham, J. H. (2007). Fundamentals of Financial Management. Thomson Learning.

35. Competition Commission South Africa. (2009). Unleashing Rivalry - Ten years of enforcement by the South African competition authorities. Pretoria: Competition Commission and Competition Tribunal.

36. Osae, W., Fauconnier, C., & Webber-Youngman, R. (2011). A value assessment of mergers and acquisitions in the South African mining industry. The Journal of The Southern African Institute of Mining and Metallurgy, 857-869.

37. Davids, E., & Yuill, D. (2008). The Mergers & Acquisitions Review - 2Ed - South Africa. Retrieved from Bowman Gilfillan: http://www.legal500.com/assets/images/stories/firmdevs/bowm51403/the_ma_review.pdf

38. Mergermarket. (2013). Deal Drivers Africa. Retrieved from Mergermarket: http://mergermarketgroup.com/wp-content/uploads/2013/12/Deal_Drivers_Africa_2013.pdf

39. Kamhunga, S. (2012, 12 04). Half of Africa's top 10 merger and aquisition deals in 2012 targeted SA . Retrieved from Business Day Live: www.bdlive.co.za/business/2012/12/04/half-of-africas-top-10-merger-and-acquisition-deals-this-year-target-sa

40. Davids, E., & Hale, A. (2012). MergersandAcquisitions-Review-2012. Retrieved from Bowman Gilfillan: http://www.bowman.co.za/FileBrowser/ArticleDocuments/MergersandAcquisitions-Review-2012.pdf

41. Hlophe, S. (2011). M&A in Africa - window of opportunity for South Africa is open. Retrieved from Ernst & Young, Africa: http://www.ey.com/ZA/en/Newsroom/News-releases/2012---Press-release---June---M-and-A-in-Africa---window-of-opportunity-for-South-Africa-is-open---but-for-how-long

42. Investopedia. (2014, 09 05). Forward Market. Retrieved from investopedia.com: http://www.investopedia.com/terms/f/forwardmarket.asp

43. StandardBank. (2014). forward foreign exchange. Retrieved from standardbank.co.za: http://ws9.standardbank.co.za/forexWebsite/docs/forward_foreign_exchange.pdf

44. Jeffrey Frankel, J. P. (2010). The forward market in emerging currencies: Less biased than in major currencies. Journal of International Money and Finance, Volume 29, Issue 3, 585-598.

45 Fischer Black, Myron S. Scholes. (1974). The Effects of Dividend Yield and Dividend Policy on Common Stock Prices and Returns, Journal of Financial Economics. May 1974, Vol. 1, Issue 1, Pages 1–22

46 Docking, Diane Scott; Koch, Paul D. (2005)." Sensitivity of investor reaction to market direction and volatility: dividend change announcements", Journal of Financial Research, Internet Paper.

www.ingramcontent.com/pod-product-compliance
Lightning Source LLC
Chambersburg PA
CBHW070330190526
45169CB00005B/1826